SCHIRMER'S LIBRARY
OF MUSICAL CLASSICS

Vol. 2120

THE CLASSICAL ERA
PIANO ALBUM

15 Favorite Pieces by

Beethoven

Haydn

Mozart

ISBN 978-1-4950-5163-0

G. SCHIRMER, *Inc.*

DISTRIBUTED BY

7777 W. BLUEMOUND RD. P.O. BOX 13819 MILWAUKEE, WI 53213

www.musicsalesclassical.com
www.halleonard.com

CONTENTS

LUDWIG VAN BEETHOVEN

Piano Sonata No. 8 in C minor, "Pathétique," Op. 13
4   Grave – Allegro di molto e con brio
14   Adagio cantabile
18   Rondo: Allegro

Piano Sonata No. 14 in C-sharp minor, "Moonlight," Op. 27, No. 2
26   Adagio sostenuto
30   Allegretto
32   Presto agitato

Piano Sonata No. 19 in G minor, Op. 49, No. 1
44   Andante
47   Rondo: Allegro

Piano Sonata No. 20 in G Major, Op. 49, No. 2
52   Allegro ma non troppo
56   Tempo di Menuetto

61   Bagatelle in A minor, "Für Elise," WoO 59

64   Six Variations on "Nel cor più non mi sento"
       from Giovanni Paisiello's *La Molinara* by Paisiello, WoO 70

FRANZ JOSEPH HAYDN

Piano Sonata in C Major, Hob. XVI:35
72   Allegro con brio
78   Adagio
80   Finale: Allegro

Piano Sonata in D Major, Hob. XVI:37
82   Allegro con brio
86   Largo e sostenuto
87   Finale: Presto, ma non troppo

Piano Sonata in E-flat Major, Hob. XVI:49
91   Allegro [non troppo]
98   Adagio cantabile
102   Finale: Tempo di Minuetto

Piano Sonata in E-flat Major, Hob. XVI:52
107   Allegro
115   Adagio
118   Finale: Presto

WOLFGANG AMADEUS MOZART

124   Twelve Variations on "Ah, vous dirai-je, Maman," K. 265

130   Fantasy in D minor, K. 397

Piano Sonata in A minor, K. 310
135   Allegro maestoso
142   Andante cantabile con espressione
148   Presto

Piano Sonata in A Major, K. 331
154   Andante grazioso
162   Menuetto – Trio
166   Rondo: Allegretto (Alla turca)

Piano Sonata in C Major, K. 545
170   Allegro
174   Andante
178   Rondo: Allegretto grazioso

to Prince Carl von Lichnowsky

PIANO SONATA
in C Minor
"Pathétique"

Ludwig van Beethoven
Op. 13

Abbreviations: M. T. signifies Main Theme; S. T., Sub-Theme; Cl. T., Closing Theme; D. G., Development-group; R., Return; Tr., Transition; Md. T., Mid-Theme; Ep., Episode.

a) The 32nd-note must be perceptibly detached from the next-following dotted sixteenth-note, and this latter sustained for its full value — a mode of execution peculiar to such rhythms in the old masters; compare Händel's Prelude to the F-minor Fugue, and Bach's Prelude to the G-minor Fugue in Part II of "The Well-tempered Clavichord."

b) This run should be performed expressively, and in the second half with a slight retardation, so as to bring out the melodic outlines.

c) Carefully observe the increasing value of the "lifting-note;" the first time, the sixth eighth in the measure is only a sixteenth-note; in the next measure, the D on the second eighth is a full eighth-note, while the F on the sixth eighth becomes a quarter-note. This effects a melodic intensification.

Allegro di molto e con brio. ($\sharp$ = 144.)

a) The relation between the movement of the *Introduction* and the *Allegro* is properly this: That a whole note in the latter is exactly equivalent to an eighth-note in the former. Consequently, the *Allegro* may be begun at the rate of M.M. $\sharp$ =132, which movement would not, however, be fast enough further on, in view of the passionate character developed.

b) In tremolo-figures like these, the player should be content to mark only such bass notes (and then only at the first stroke) as indicate a new progression in the harmony.

c) The direction *agitato* also calls for a *non legato* as strict as possible, which, of course, must not impair the evenness of the movement.

a) Although this *"second"* subject, too, is passionately agitated, the unvarying tempestuous sweep of the first cannot be kept up throughout. Play the first measure of each four-measure period — the preluding bass — somewhat more quietly, the following three with all the more animation; shade the 16 measures in Eb-minor differently from the parallel passage in Db-major; in short, invest the entire dialogue with the most varied coloring possible.

b) Execution: ![graphic] according to the familiar rule, that all graces take their value from, and are played within, the value of the principal note.

c) Execution: ![graphic] according to the same rule; beware of the facile and tasteless triplet in eighth-notes, to which even the anticipated passing shake would be preferable, though against the rules.

a) These first 4 measures are to be played without the least retardation, yet very quietly, and with no accentuation of the accompaniment.

a) The hold (pause) must be sustained precisely 3 measures, so as to form another 4-measure period.

But a quarter-rest should precede the reprise of the first division:

b) Retard the entrance of the B in the bass, in order to enhance the pleasurable suspense attendant upon the enharmonic change of the diminished chord of the seventh in the transition from G-minor to E-minor; and play the following passage throughout with full dreamy freedom.

a) Despite the identity of this phrase with that in meas. 5 of the first *Grave,* it must now be played with a wholly different expression — or, rather, with none whatever, this being rendered necessary by the doubled rapidity of the movement (♪ in the *Grave* = o in the *Allegro*).

b) Although the phrasing ⟐ etc. would more nearly correspond to the original form of this passage in meas. 7 *et seq.* of the so-called second subject (E♭-minor), it would not be in keeping with the general (progressional) character of the development-section.

c) The player should slightly sustain the several tones ⟐ but not so as to make the movement heavy.

a) As an exception to the rule, this trill must not begin on the auxiliary, so as not to blur the melodic

outlines; seven notes ♪♪♪♪♪♪♪ vigorously played suffice in such rapid tempo

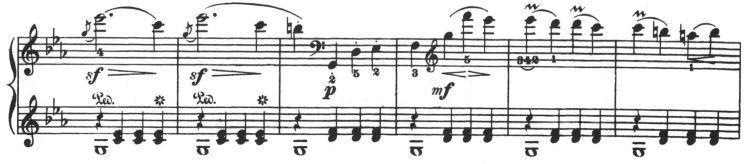

a) This *piano* must enter abruptly, which requires some practice, especially with the left hand; similarly in the parallel passage 4 measures further on.

a) In the original the *decrescendo* begins at this measure, which seems to us rather too prolonged for 6 full measures, — the more so, because an actual *forte* would be inadmissible in the preceding; for this reason we consider a *poco cresc.* more suitable for the first two measures.

b) Take care not to play E♭ instead of F in the right hand, as a C-minor chord is out of the question here; the C in both Soprano and Bass is simply a passing-note of the dominant chord.

a) Sustain the hold (pause) 3 full measures (comp. {Note a, the first holds in the *Grave* have precisely the same dura- {Page 118); tion (subtracting the 32nd-note).

b) The bass note on the third fourth-note must have a penetrating and prolonged tone, in order to be quite audible through the seventh eighth-note as the root of the chord of the sixth.

c) This coda cannot be played too rapidly.

d) It is best not to use the pedal with these chords.

a) To the best of our knowledge no one has yet remarked the striking affinity of the theme of this movement, even with reference to its external melodic structure, to that of one of the loftiest *Adagios* of grandest scope from the Master's last period; — we mean the *Adagio* of the Ninth Symphony, written almost a quarter of a century later. The performance of both demands an equally inspired mood. The player's task, to "make his fingers sing," may perhaps necessitate a more frequent use of the pedal than we have indicated, which must of course be controlled by a most watchful ear.

b) This first middle section of the Rondo (for such this *Adagio* is in form) may be taken slightly *meno andante*, i. e., slower; but no more so than needful (so as not to drag), and, therefore, in only a few places.

c) The turns in this and the next measure should not commence with, but immediately after, a sixteenth-note in the bass,

thus: [musical notation] and: [musical notation]

a) A tasteful execution of this grace is impossible in strict time. An abbreviation of the first two principal notes (C and B♭) being quite as impracticable as a shifting of the inverted mordent into the preceding measure as an unaccented appoggiatura, the measure must simply be extended by an additional 32nd-note.

b) In this repetition of the theme, the left hand may be allowed to play a more expressive part; and, on the whole, a somewhat lighter shading of the melody is now admissible by way of contrast to the following (gloomier) middle section.

c) The ascending diminished fifth may be phrased, as it were, like a question, to which the succeeding bass figure may be regarded as the answer.

a) It appears advisable slightly to hasten this measure and the next, and then to retard the third not inconsiderably; the former on account of the cessation in the harmonic advance, the latter by reason of the varied modulation, which must be quite free from disquieting haste in its return to the theme.

b) Though strictly subordinated to the melody, the triplets should be brought out with animated distinctness.

c) The two 32nd-notes in the melody may very properly be sounded with the last note of the triplet of 16th-notes in the accompaniment; whereas a mathematically exact division would probably confuse both parts.

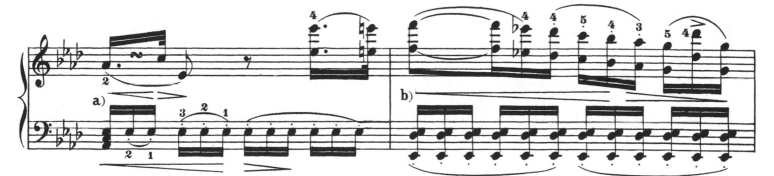

a) Execute like a triplet:

b) In the original, the shading of this passage is marked differently from that two measures before, the *diminuendo* already beginning with C, and not with A♭ as here marked. This latter nuance — the prolongation of the *crescendo* — appeals to our feeling as the more delicate, "more tenderly passionate," to quote Richard Wagner's happy remark on the "Interpretation of Beethoven".

c) Mark the separation of the slurs in this figure and those following; the six notes sound trivial if slurred together.

Rondo.

Allegro. ($\quart=96$.)

a) Although this third movement is less "pathetic" than the preceding ones, the player alone will be to blame should the Pathetic Sonata end apathetically. The original, to be sure, contains only the most indispensable expression-marks, which it has been the aim of our Edition to supplement efficiently; as, for example, by the *crescendo* ending *piano* in measures 2-3, by emphasizing the distinction to be made, in the figures for the left hand, between the parts (tones) which are essential (independent) organic elements, and those which are mere harmonic filling; etc.

b) In executing this grace, the player must be careful not to produce the effect of parallel octaves with the bass (F-A♭, and in the next measure E♭-G); rather than this, the slide might be treated as an appendage to the foregoing notes.

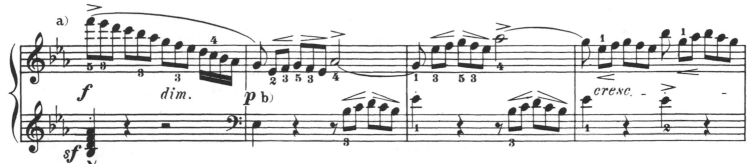

a) There can hardly be a doubt that the Master was compelled, by the restricted compass of the keyboard of his day (only up to F³), to content himself with the fifth of the dominant chord, instead of rising to the higher seventh (A♭) as in the three other parallel passages. A change in conformity with his original intention is impracticable, however, because the ensuing measure would then be made to lie an octave higher, and would sound somewhat thin for the first time (it is immediately repeated in the octave).

b) These imitations, although *piano,* must be played with great animation, and not in that characterless *legato* which might be called anti-symphonic.

c) The preceding Remark applies equally to this and similar passages.

a) The fingering given by us serves to aid in executing this run with the exact rhythmic divisions desired by the composer. The hold which follows appears really superfluous; for, by the prolongation of the chord through $1\frac{1}{4}$ measures, all demands of the pulsing rhythm ___ which goes on even during the rests of a piece ___ are fully met.

a) The tempo, of course, remains the same, but free from any fluctuating agitation. Observe, that the theme "proper" begins with an ascending fourth; consequently, the left hand should be slightly emphasized in the fifth and sixth measures. This holds good for meas. 13, 14, etc.

b) The mark **ff** is set rather early, in view of the fact, that the intensification continues through the next six measures. For this reason, the player will do well to husband his strength at first.

a) The more tempestuously the 12 preceding measures have been played, the longer may this hold (see Note a, page 160) be sustained.

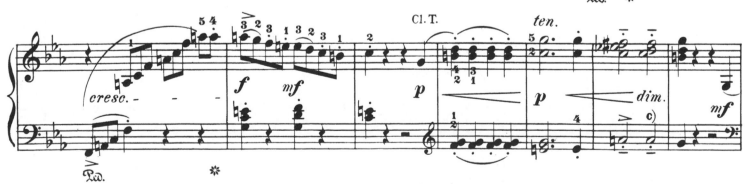

a) The second subject must be played more delicately and quietly here than at its first entrance in E♭ major.

b) A collision of the two parts on D² must be avoided by anticipating the right hand by an arpeggio in the

left, lifting the left-hand thumb instantly after the stroke; thus:

c) The second note in the bass might, in conformity with the parallel passages in the first division, be A♭.

a) These next **13 measures** should be played with considerable freedom as regards tempo, and with a decided independent stress on the lower part in the left hand. Special attention should be paid to the composer's directions concerning both the shading of meas. 6-7 and 8-9, and their phrasing, which is not in one-measure rhythm (as the motive at the first glance apparently invites), but in two-measure rhythm. In proportion to the greater or lesser degree of passion put forth by the player before the *calando*, this latter is to be conceived as a *diminuendo* and *ritardando*. Excess in either direction is, of course, reprehensible.

b) Particularly note the *Auftakt* (fractional initial measure) in the bass, here representing the regular introduction. By playing the theme wholly without shading on its fourth (and last) appearance, the close is well prepared and led up to.

a) Moderate the tempo on commencing this measure, in order that the ensuing run can be executed precisely according to the given divisions and without the least retardation. The following hold may be sustained very long—as long as the sonority of the piano permits.

b) A *ritardando* in this epilogue would be in bad taste; the tempo must be strictly sustained to the close.

c) The $\boldsymbol{fff}$ is found in all the old Editions,—almost the sole instance where this superlative, surely as frequently intended as rarely used is employed by the Master. Hence follows the necessity of an unusually powerful *crescendo* in the preceding run.

to Countess Julia Guicciardi

PIANO SONATA

in C-sharp minor
"Moonlight"

Ludwig van Beethoven
Op. 27, No. 2

Abbreviations: M. T. signifies Main Theme; S. T., Sub-Theme; Cl. T., Closing Theme; D. G., Development-group; R., Return; Tr., Transition; Md. T., Mid-Theme; Ep., Episode.

a) It is evident that the highest part, as the melody, requires a firmer touch than the accompanying triplet-figure; and the first note in the latter must never produce the effect of a doubling of the melody in the lower octave.

b) A more frequent use of the pedal than is marked by the editor, and limited here to the most essential passages, is allowable; it is not advisable, however, to take the original directions *sempre senza sordini* (i. e., without dampers) too literally.

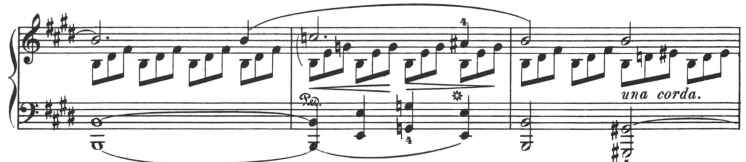

a) The player must guard against carrying his hand back with over-anxious haste. For, in any event, a strict pedantic observance of time is out of place in this period, which has rather the character of an improvisation.

a) The notes with a dash above them may properly be dwelt upon in such a way as to give them the effect of suspensions, e. g., [music example]: in fact, a utilization of the inner parts, in accordance with the laws of euphony and the course of the modulation, is recommended throughout the piece.

II. Allegretto. a) (♩. = 56.)

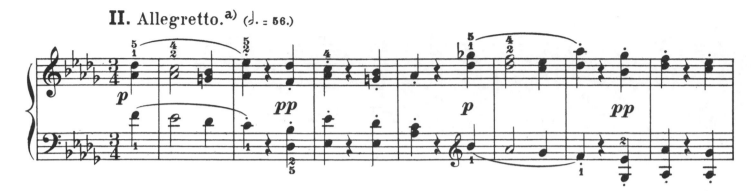

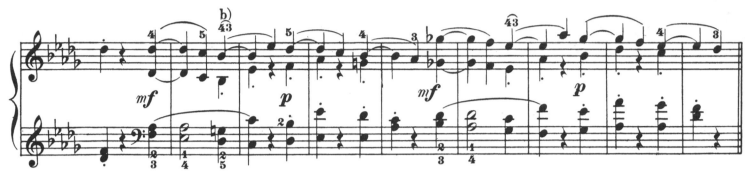

a) *Allegretto* means *poco allegro*. The movement should not exceed a moderate minuet-tempo, in this point precisely resembling the analogous movements in the Sonatas Op. 2, Nos 1 and 2; Op. 10, No 2; Op. 14, No 1, not to speak of later ones. This anti-Scherzo is, indeed, a lyrical Intermezzo between two tragical Nocturnes. Franz Liszt's clever *mot: "Une fleur entre deux abîmes"* (a flower betwixt two abysses) gives the key to the true interpretation.

b) Special care must be bestowed on the twofold task of the right hand — a songful leading of the melody, with a light and graceful *staccato* in the second part, which latter combines with the left-hand part as a third factor.

a) A very common amateurish error — which, we regret to say, is countenanced here and in other places by Herr Lebert's otherwise so meritorious edition — is the notion that a closer *legato* is obtainable, in descending octave-passages, by a change of fingers. Precisely the opposite effect is produced by the following manipulation: ; the higher part, the one most strongly affecting the ear, suffers a most sensible interruption. A slight muscular stretching of the palm of the hand, which is no harder to learn than shifting on a stringed instrument, will amply fulfil all requirements.

b) An undelayed attack (of the Finale) is quite as indispensable to the general effect as in the two reprises preceding.

III. Presto agitato. (♩=88.)

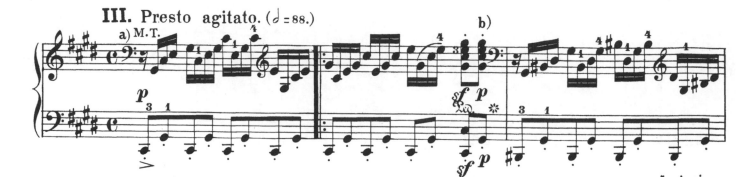

a) This passage, up to the abrupt stroke on the fourth beat in measure 2, must be played with almost ethereal lightness in the very smoothest *piano*, and (if only for the sake of distinctness) as little *legato* as is in any way compatible with the great rapidity of the movement.

b) The second stroke has only the significance of an echo, the repercussion of the first. In measure 8 it is different, owing to its leading over to new matter.

a) This grace is written out in conformity with its undeviating mode of execution. Avoid a repeated accentuation of the lowest bass note; an accent is needful only on its first entrance.

b) The rapid movement, conjoined with required exertion of strength, hardly admits of a longer trill

than:

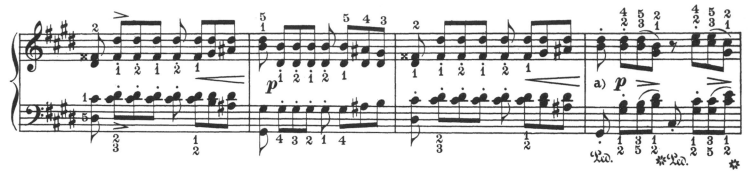

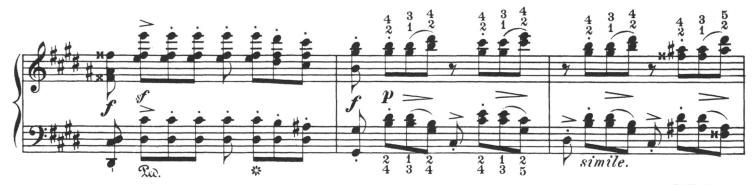

a) These thirds can be brought out with perfect distinctness only by means of this fingering, troublesome though it be.

b) It is self-evident that a hammering-out of these "passionate" eighth-notes in strict time would be incorrect in an æsthetic sense. By playing the first half of the measure with stronger emphasis (and hence greater freedom), as is demanded in particular by the peculiar rhythmic importance of the second eighth-note, and somewhat accelerating the second half, both the unity of the measure as such, and also the psychical agitation, receive due consideration. **c)** This melodic phrase, whose performance demands the intensest feeling, is probably to be understood thus: i.e., more singingly sustained than the marking denotes.

a) The literal execution is:

b) The repetition prescribed here according to custom impresses us as a chilling tautology.

c) This movement-figure, like the similar one in the right hand 4 measures further on, must be played entirely without accentuation; only in the principal modulations, e. g., the transition from F♯-minor to G-major and back, individual characteristic intervals may be slightly emphasized. On the other hand, a transformation of the figures into an indistinct *tremolo* would, of course, be wholly out of place.

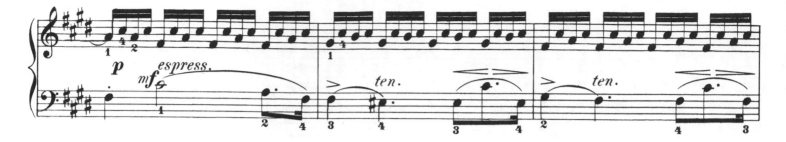

a) In the analogous passage in the first division, this period embraces 4 measures, whereas it has but 3 here. There is no reason why either should be altered for the sake of symmetry of pattern. Both are good, and greater brevity and conciseness in form are æsthetically justified in repetitions.

CODA.
animato.

Tempo I.

a) This second hold (*pause*) may be sustained longer than the preceding. Further, a slight rest must intervene (for acoustic reasons, apart from æsthetic ones) before the reentrance of the first subject, as is indicated by a ⌢ over the bar.

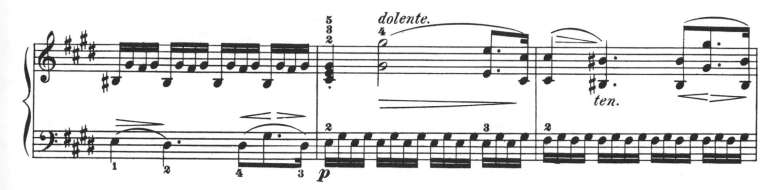

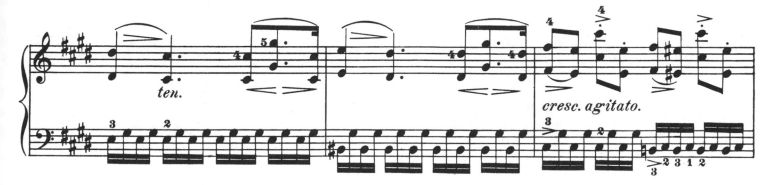

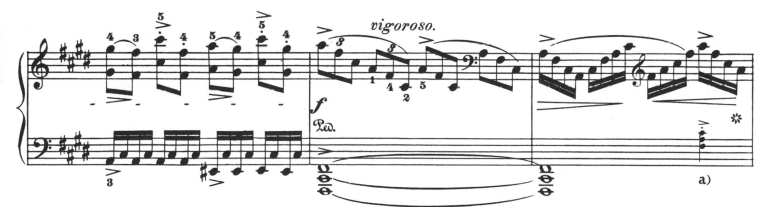

a) There is no irreverence, even to the letter of the composer's work, in enhancing — in analogy with the D-minor Sonata Op. 31 Nº 2 — the accent marked on the fourth beat by a chord struck with the left hand.

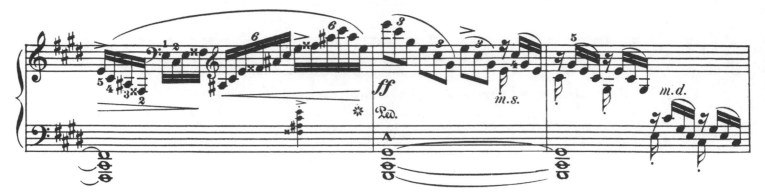

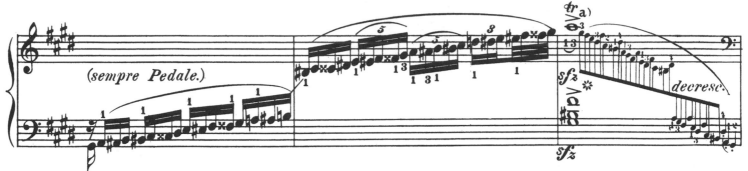

Tempo I, ma tranquillo.

Adagio.   **b)**

a) The editor performs this cadenza with the following rhythmic divisions, the required *ritardando* then result-

ing as a matter of course:

b) *Adagio:* twice as slow as the *Presto* - movement, but not slower.

c) Avoid a *crescendo* in the preceding measures; the *forte* must enter with instantaneous abruptness, giving us a reproduction of the principal divisions in miniature — the deep melancholy of the *Adagio*, the wild despe ration of the *Finale*.

PIANO SONATA
in G minor

Ludwig van Beethoven
Op. 49, No. 1

Abbreviations: M. T., signifies Main Theme; S. T., Sub Theme; Cl. T., Closing Theme; D. G., Development-group; R., Return; Tr., Transition; Md. T., Mid-Theme; Ep., Episode; App., Appendix.

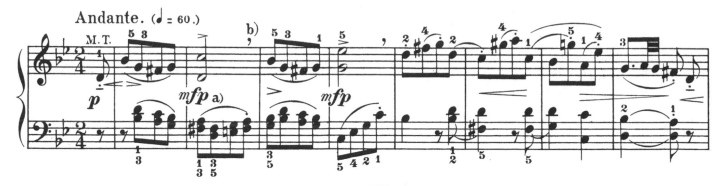

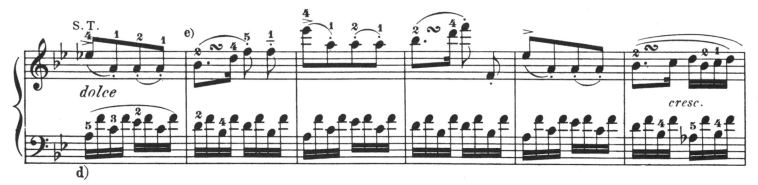

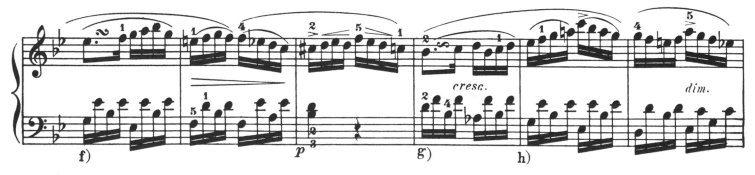

a) *mfp* signifies: the first note *mf*, the following ones *p*.

b) With the comma we indicate places where the player must perceptibly mark the end of a rhythmic group or section, by lifting the last note just before its time-value expires, although the composer wrote no rest.

c) (music example)

d) The left hand more subdued than the right, but still accenting the first of each pair of 16th-notes (i. e.: the bass notes proper) somewhat more than the second.

e) (music example)

f) Here and in the next measure the left hand should accent only the first note in each group of 16th-notes somewhat more than the others, but in all cases less than the soprano.

g) As at d.)

h) In these three measures as at f.)

a) As at (**f**) on the preceding Page

b)

c) The left hand here again more subdued than the right.

d) As at (**a**).

e) In these twelve measures the first and third notes in each group of 16th notes should be made somewhat more prominent than the other notes, yet always in subordination to the melody, excepting the tones marked ＞

a) From here through the next 6 measures the left hand, having the melody, should predominate over the right, and, where it has 2 tones, chiefly accentuate the higher one.

b) As on first Page.

c) The next 5 measures as on first Page.

d) Doubtless literally meant neither for ⨾⨾ nor for: ⨾⨾ but ⨾⨾

e) This and the following turns again as on first Page.

f) From here onward as on second Page.

Rondo.
Allegro. (♩. = 92.)

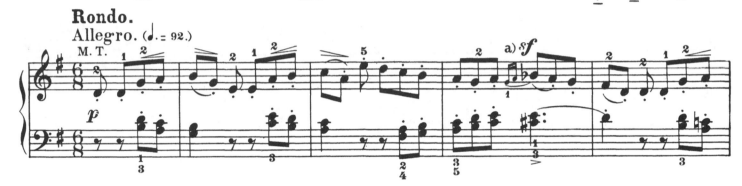

a)

b) Proceed only after a rest.

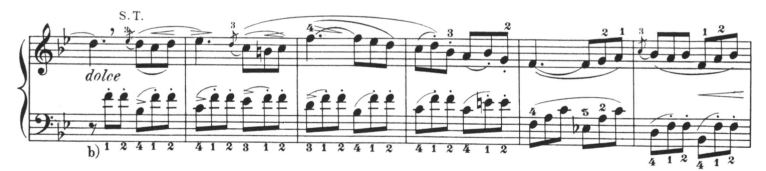

a) In these groups of 16th-notes, accent each first note slightly more than the 5 following, while subordinating all to the soprano. These same accented notes, too, (except in the fourth measure) should be held down during the second 16th-note.

b) Also subordinate this accompaniment, but accent the first note of each triplet, as the bass note proper, a trifle more than the other two.

a) [musical notation example]

b) Here, of course, only the first eighth-note in each measure should be accented.

a) From here up to the *ff* discreetly subordinate the left hand throughout (also in the repetitions of the fundamental tone.)

b) Let the *ff* enter abruptly with the fourth eighth-note, without any previous *crescendo*.

PIANO SONATA
in G Major

Ludwig van Beethoven
Op. 49, No. 2

Abbreviations: M.T. signifies Main Theme; S.T., Sub-Theme; Cl. T., Closing Theme; D.G., Development-Group; R., Return; Tr., Transition; Md. T. Mid-Theme; Ep., Episode.

Allegro ma non troppo. (♩ = 132.)

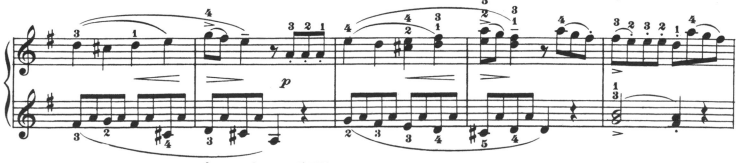

a) Strike all short appoggiaturas on the beat, simultaneously with the accompaniment-note.

b) F♯ should be executed as a long, accented appoggiatura:

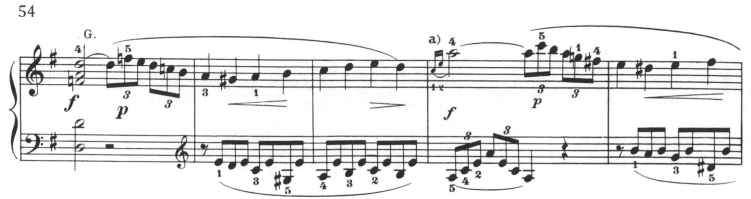

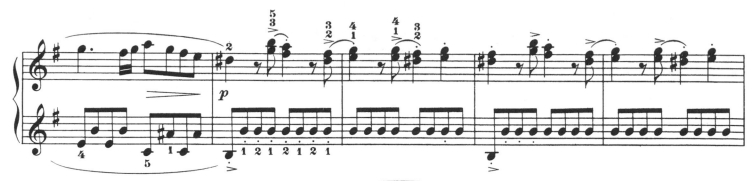

a)

Tempo di Menuetto. ($\bullet$ = 112.)

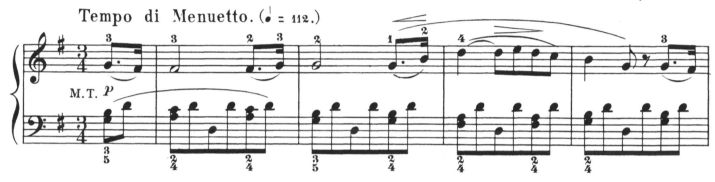

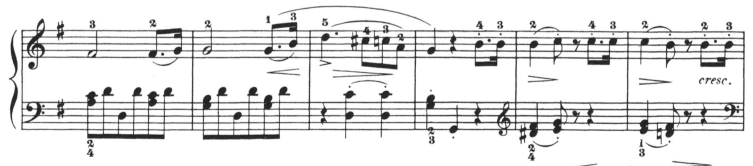

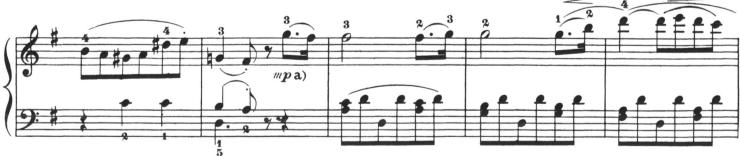

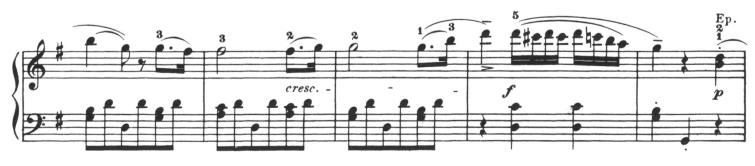

a) *mp* (*mezzo piano*, moderately soft) signifies a degree of tone-power midway between *p* and *mf*.

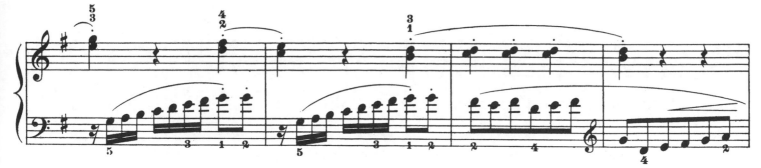

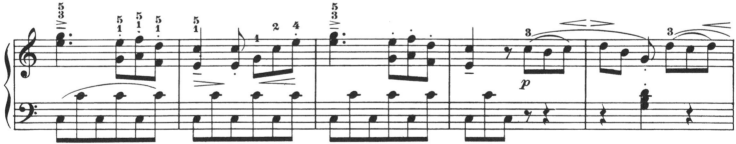

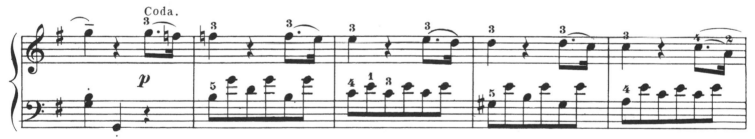

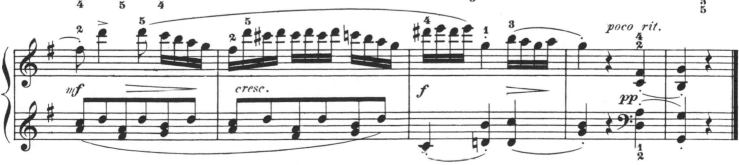

BAGATELLE
in A minor
"Für Elise"

Ludwig van Beethoven
WoO 59

Poco moto

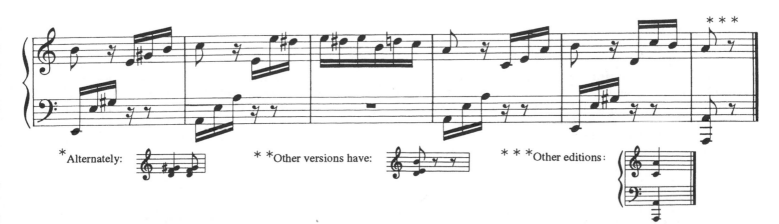

*Alternately: * *Other versions have: * * *Other editions:

SIX VARIATIONS

on "Nel cor più non mi sento" from Giovanni Paisiello's *La Molinara*

Edited by Sigmund Lebert

Ludwig van Beethoven
WoO 70

(a) Always strike the appoggiatura-note simultaneously with the first accompaniment - note, somewhat shortly, yet without impairing clearness. The accent falls, however, not on the appoggiatura, but on the principal note.

(b) The alterations given by us in small notes, aim at making these variations easily playable by small hands, which cannot yet stretch an octave.

(c) Continue from this movement to the following without interruption of the measure, except when the contrary is indicated by a fermata over the closing double-bar.

Var. I

(a) Such a comma indicates a breaking-off somewhat sooner, and a subsequent fresh attack.

(b) *rit.*

Var. II

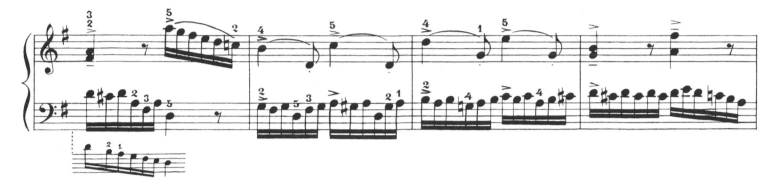

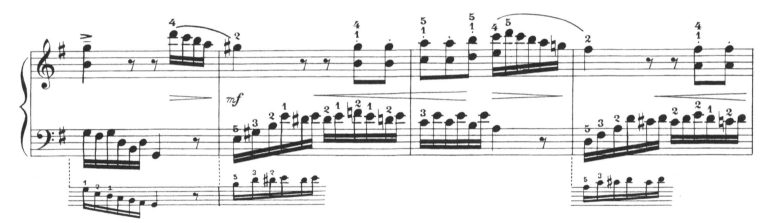

Var. III

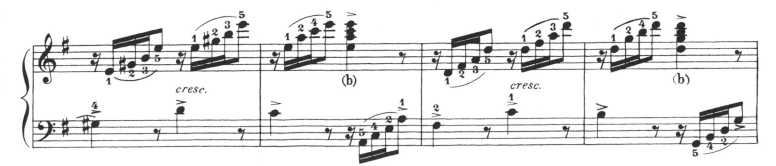

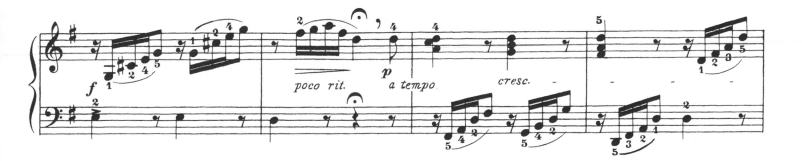

(a) Emphasize the left hand somewhat here, as it has the principal notes of the melody.

(b) Small hands must leave out the lowest tone.

Poco più tranquillo (♪=144)

Var. IV

(a) Both the *d-b* in the left hand, as also the *g* in the right, are to be held during the execution of the small notes.

Var. V.

Un pochettino più animato ($\bullet\!\!\cdot = 60$)

Var. VI

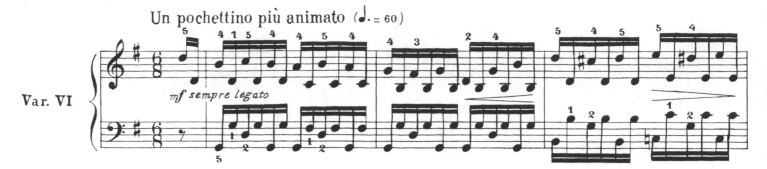

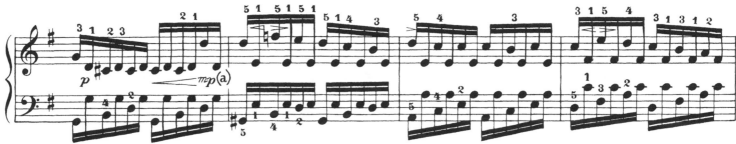

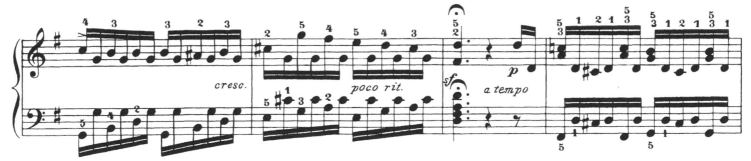

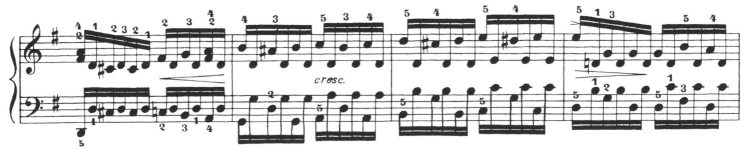

(a) *mp* (*mezzo piano*, rather softly) signifies a degree of tone-power between *p* and *mf*

to the sisters Caterina and Marianna von Auenbrugger

PIANO SONATA
in C Major

Franz Joseph Haydn
Hob. XVI:35

Allegro con brio

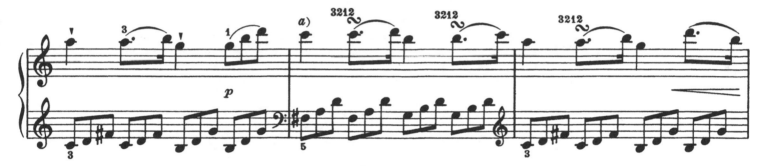

a)

Adagio Tempo I

Adagio

a)    b)

Finale
Allegro

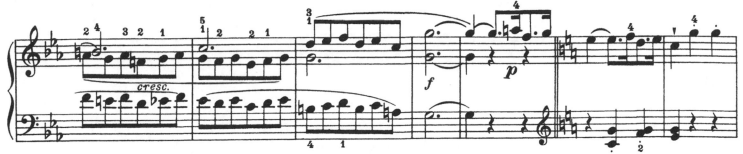

to the sisters Caterina and Marianna von Auenbrugger

PIANO SONATA
in D Major

Franz Joseph Haydn
Hob. XVI:37

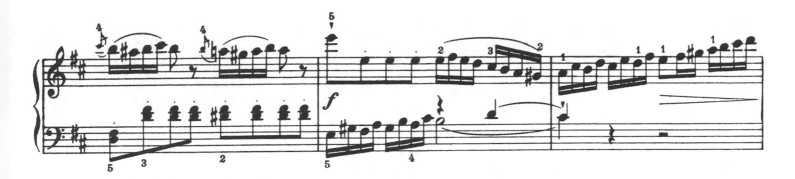

a) = ⚬⚬

Largo e sostenuto

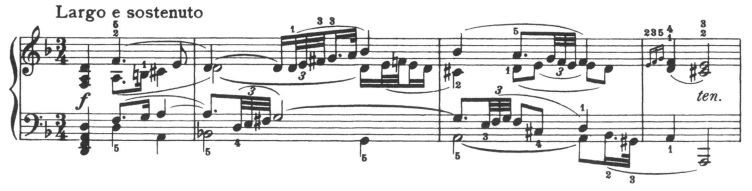

Attacca subito
il Finale

Finale
Presto, ma non troppo

for Frau von Genzinger

PIANO SONATA
in E-flat Major

Franz Joseph Haydn
Hob. XVI:49

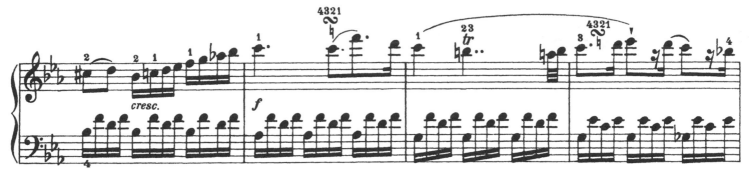

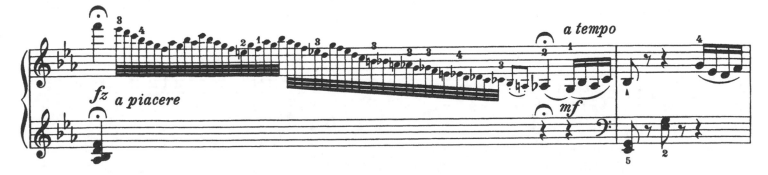

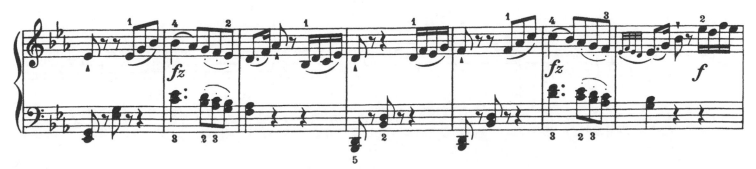

Adagio cantabile

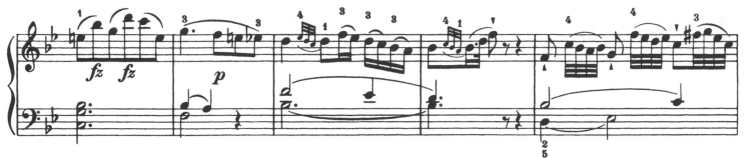

a) ... b) Original: *forz.* c) ...

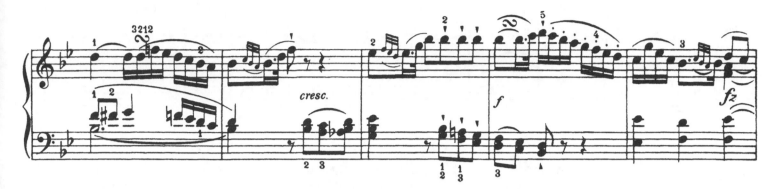

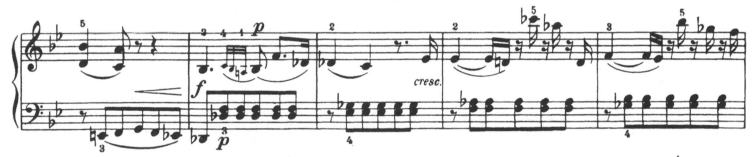

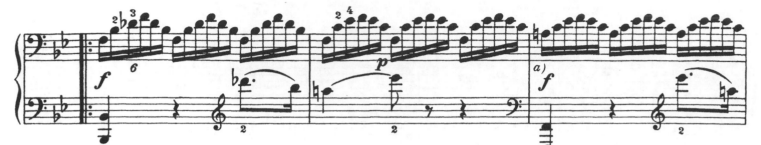

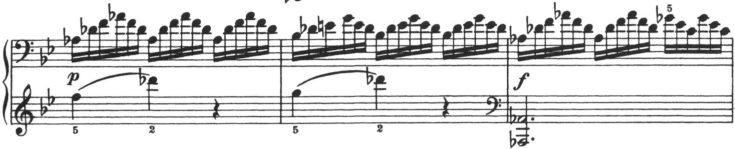

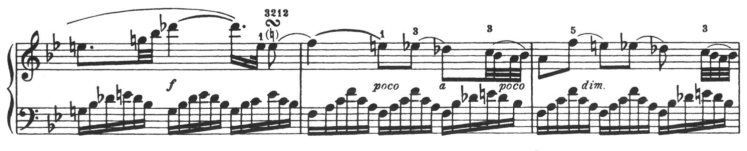

a) Original: *fz*

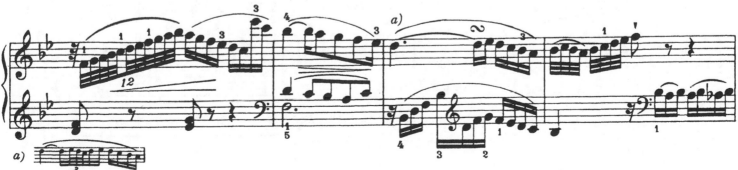

Finale
Tempo di Minuetto

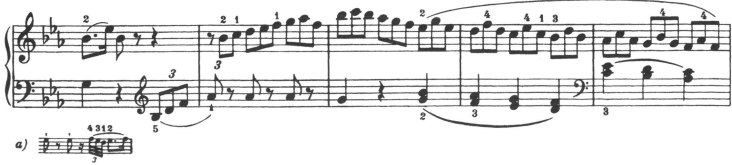

a)

to Magdalene von Kurzbeck

PIANO SONATA
in E-flat Major

Franz Joseph Haydn
Hob. XVI:52

Allegro

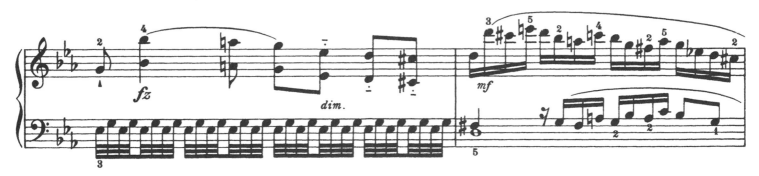

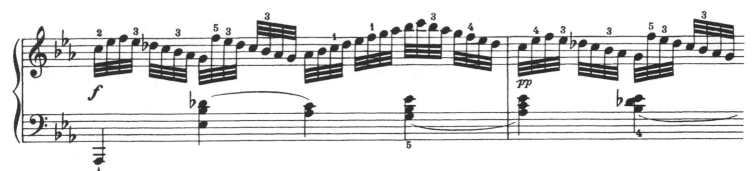

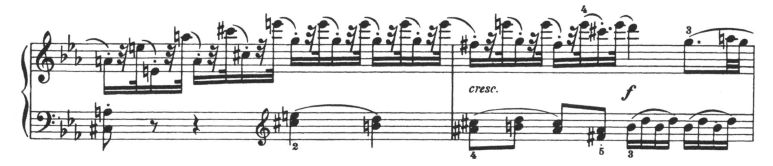

Adagio

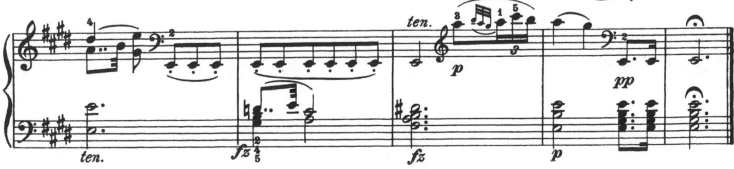

Finale
Presto

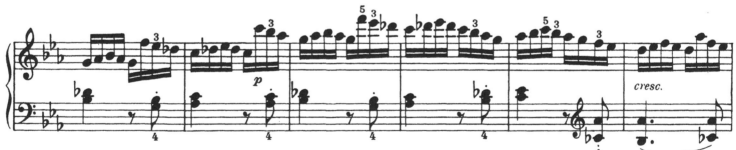

a)

a) ad libitum

Adagio

Tempo I

TWELVE VARIATIONS
on "Ah, vous dirai-je, Maman"

Wolfgang Amadeus Mozart
K. 265

(**Moderato**)

VAR. I

VAR. II

VAR. V

VAR. VI

VAR.VII

VAR.VIII
Minore

VAR.IX
Maggiore

VAR.X

VAR.XI
Adagio

VAR. XII
Allegro

FANTASY
in D minor

Wolfgang Amadeus Mozart
K. 397

PIANO SONATA
in A minor

Edited, revised and fingered by
Richard Epstein

Wolfgang Amadeus Mozart
K. 310

Allegro maestoso (♩ = 116)

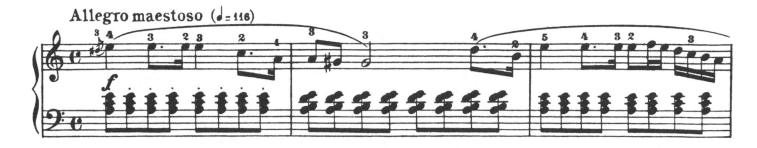

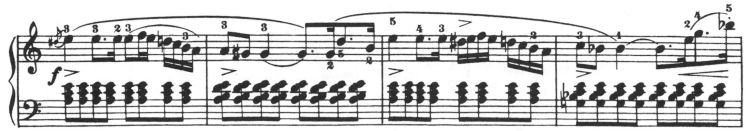

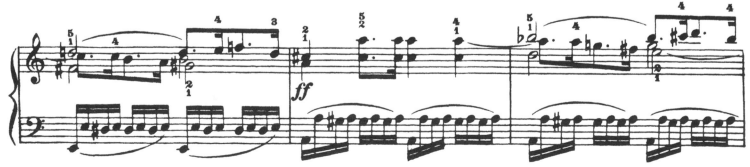

a)

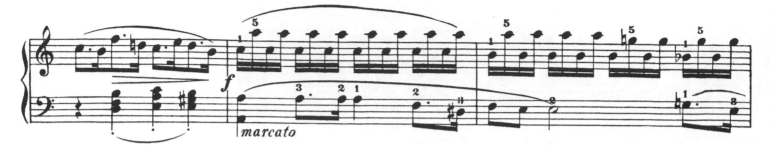

Andante cantabile con espressione (♩= 96)

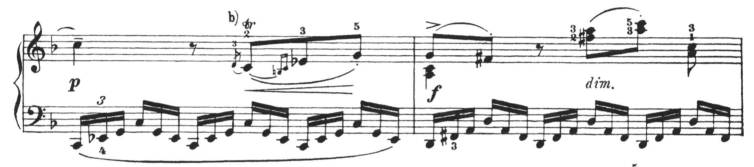

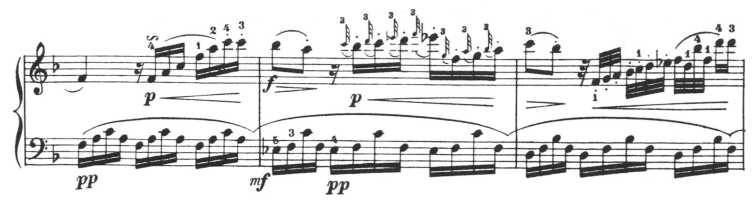

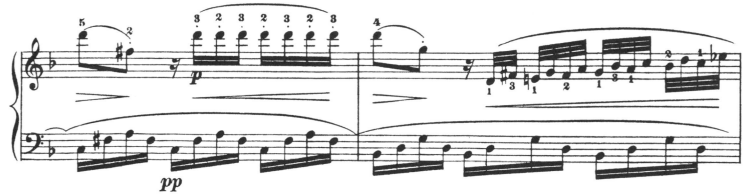

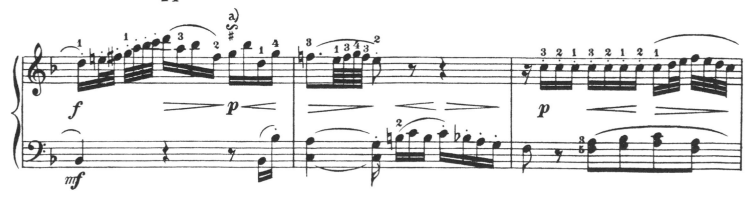

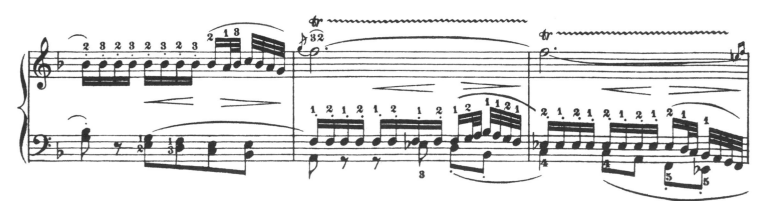

a)

Presto (♩=92)

a)

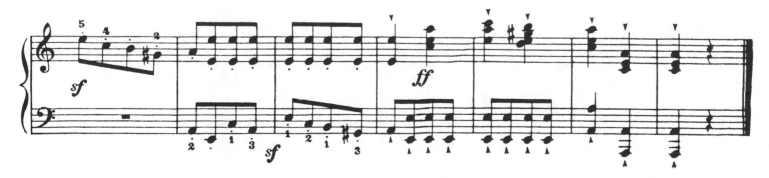

PIANO SONATA
in A Major

Edited, revised and fingered by
Richard Epstein

Wolfgang Amadeus Mozart
K. 331

Tema
Andante grazioso (♪ = 120)

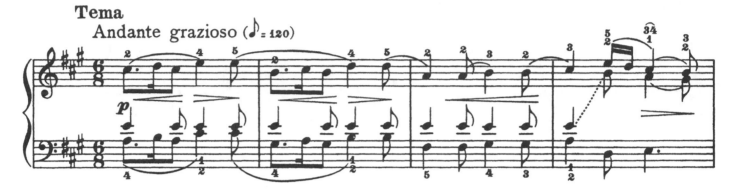

Var. I

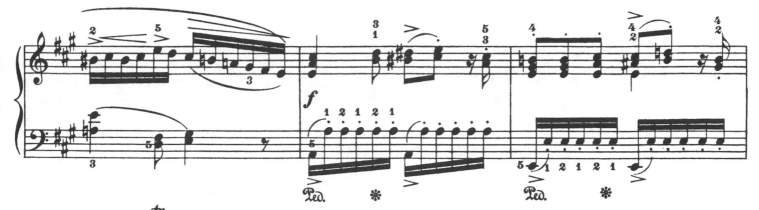

Var. II

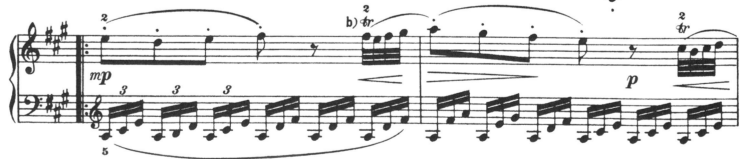

Var. III (♪ = 112)

Minore

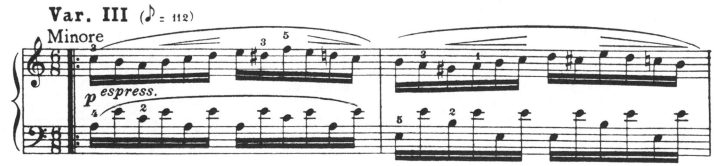

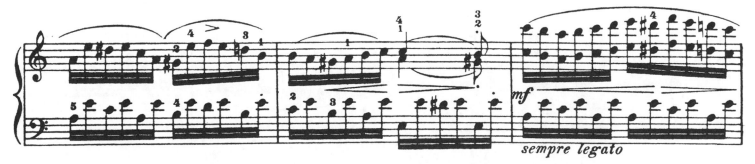

Var. IV (♪ = 120)

Maggiore

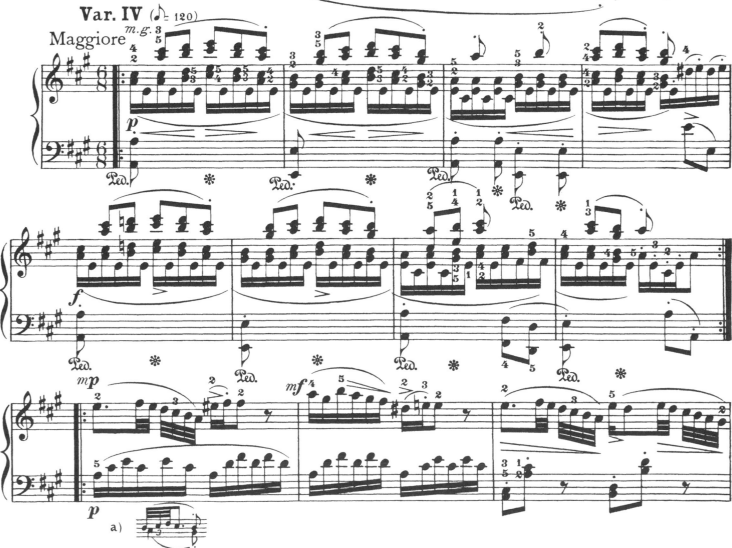

Var. V

Adagio (♪ = 60)

a)

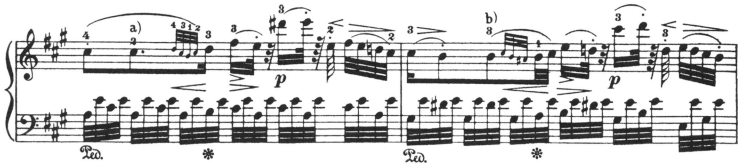

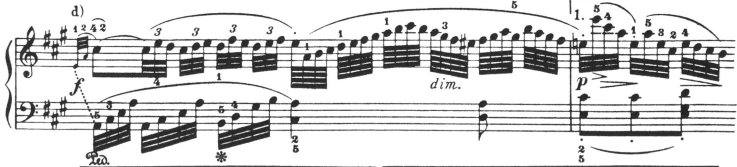

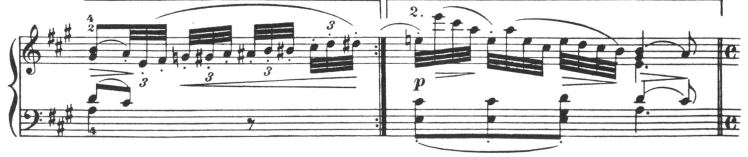

Var. VI
Allegro (♩ = 116)

a) The C sharp must enter with the bass note of the left hand.

Menuetto (♩ = 116)

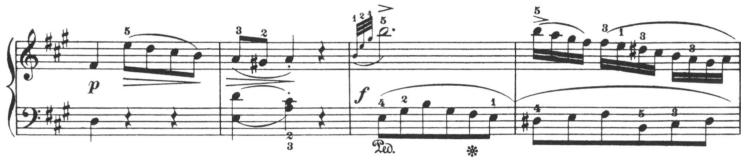

Trio

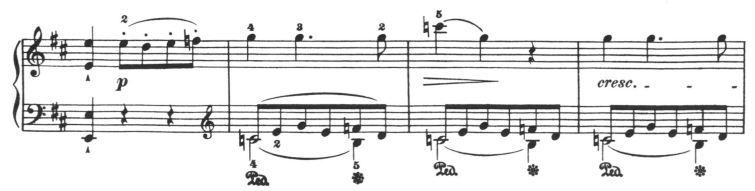

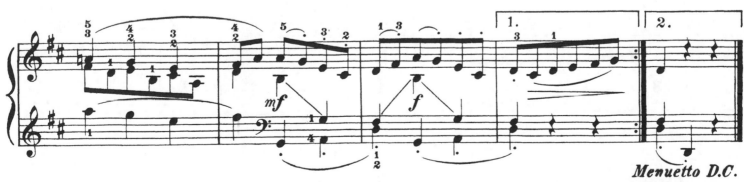

Menuetto D.C.

Alla turca
Allegretto (♩=126)

Rondo

a) Play the four notes in either hand simultaneously.

b)

PIANO SONATA
in C Major

Edited, revised and fingered by
Richard Epstein

Wolfgang Amadeus Mozart
K. 545

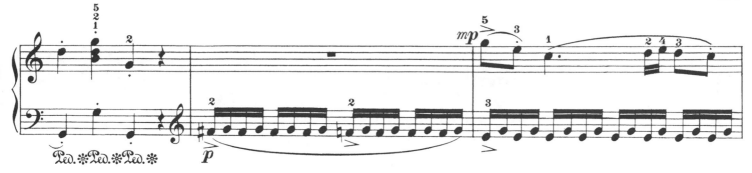

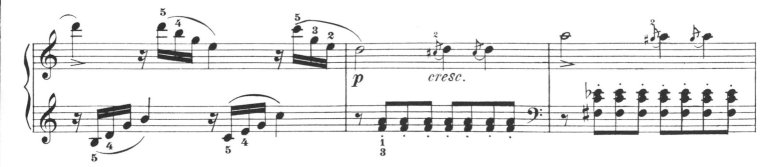

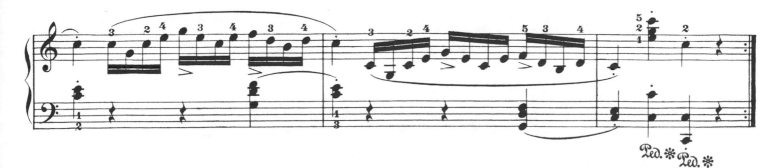

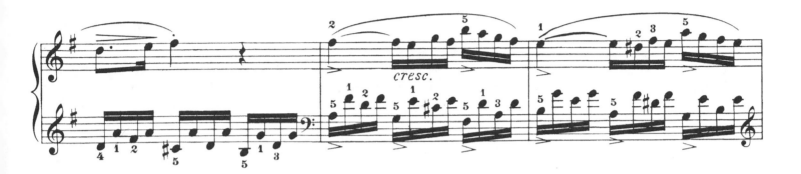

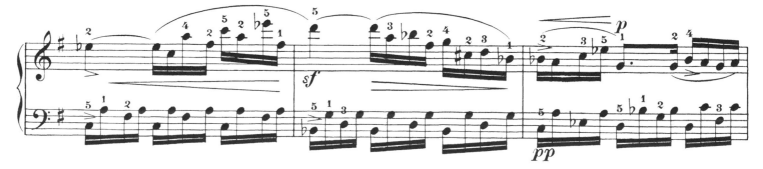

Rondo

Allegretto grazioso (♩ = 104)

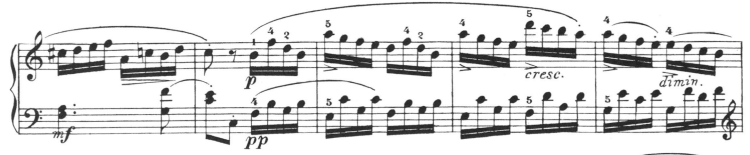